SPORTS
CHAMPIONSHIPS

THE SUPER BOWL

BY ALLAN MOREY

TORQUE
TM

BELLWETHER MEDIA · MINNEAPOLIS, MN

Are you ready to take it to the extreme? Torque books thrust you into the action-packed world of sports, vehicles, mystery, and adventure. These books may include dirt, smoke, fire, and chilling tales. **WARNING**: read at your own risk.

This edition first published in 2019 by Bellwether Media, Inc.

No part of this publication may be reproduced in whole or in part without written permission of the publisher. For information regarding permission, write to Bellwether Media, Inc., Attention: Permissions Department, 6012 Blue Circle Drive, Minnetonka, MN 55343.

Library of Congress Cataloging-in-Publication Data

Names: Morey, Allan, author.
Title: The Super Bowl / by Allan Morey.
Description: Minneapolis, Minnesota : Bellwether Media, Inc., 2019. | Series: Torque: Sports Championships | Includes bibliographical references and index. | Audience: Ages: 7-12. | Audience: Grades: 3 through 7.
Identifiers: LCCN 2018001767 (print) | LCCN 2018003383 (ebook) | ISBN 9781626178663 (hardcover : alk. paper) | ISBN 9781618914866 (paperback : alk. paper) | ISBN 9781681036076 (ebook)
Subjects: LCSH: Super Bowl–History–Juvenile literature. | Football–United States–History–Juvenile literature.
Classification: LCC GV956.2.S8 (ebook) | LCC GV956.2.S8 M67 2019 (print) | DDC 796.332/648–dc23
LC record available at https://lccn.loc.gov/2018001767

Editor: Rebecca Sabelko   Designer: Jon Eppard

Printed in the United States of America, North Mankato, MN.

TABLE OF CONTENTS

SUPER BOWL 52

It is Super Bowl 52. The Philadelphia Eagles lead the New England Patriots 38–33.

Patriots quarterback Tom Brady hopes to lead his team to score the winning touchdown. But on a passing play, Eagles defensive lineman Brandon Graham knocks the ball out of his hands. Fumble! The Eagles get the ball. They go on to win their first Super Bowl 41–33!

TOM BRADY ········>

BRANDON
GRAHAM

5 AND 5

The Patriots have
been to the Super
Bowl a record ten
times. They have five
wins and five losses.

WHAT IS THE SUPER BOWL?

The Super Bowl is the championship game for the National Football League (NFL). It is played at the end of every football season

THE BOLD NORTH

Super Bowl 52 was the coldest Super Bowl ever! The temperature at kickoff was only 2 degrees Fahrenheit (-17 degrees Celsius).

The game takes place on the first Sunday in February. It is one of the coldest months of the year. Teams often play in stadiums with roofs. Players and fans are protected from the winter weather.

The Vince Lombardi Trophy is awarded to the winner of the Super Bowl. Lombardi was the coach who led the Green Bay Packers from 1959 to 1967.

◄······ **VINCE LOMBARDI TROPHY**

VINCE LOMBARDI

Lombardi coached the Packers to win Super Bowls 1 and 2. In 1970, the NFL named the trophy in honor of him.

HISTORY OF THE SUPER BOWL

Beginning in 1960, there were two football leagues. There was the NFL and the American Football League (AFL). The NFL had 13 teams, and the AFL had 8.

The leagues were rivals. They fought over fans and players. They argued over which league played better football. Many team owners thought it cost too much to have two different leagues.

11

Soon, NFL and AFL owners came to an agreement. The winner of each league would play in a championship game.

The first Super Bowl was played on January 15, 1967. The NFL's Green Bay Packers beat the AFL's Kansas City Chiefs 35 - 10.

SUPER BOWL CHAMPS

PITTSBURGH STEELERS

SUPER BOWL 9: Steelers 16, Minnesota Vikings 6
SUPER BOWL 10: Steelers 21, Dallas Cowboys 17
SUPER BOWL 13: Steelers 35, Dallas Cowboys 31
SUPER BOWL 14: Steelers 31, Los Angeles Rams 19
SUPER BOWL 30: Steelers 17, Dallas Cowboys 27
SUPER BOWL 40: Steelers 21, Seattle Seahawks 10
SUPER BOWL 43: Steelers 27, Arizona Cardinals 23
SUPER BOWL 45: Steelers 25, Green Bay Packers 31

NFL MVP

Quarterback Terry Bradshaw helped the Pittsburgh Steelers win four Super Bowls. He was awarded Most Valuable Player twice.

TERRY BRADSHAW

ROAD TO THE SUPER BOWL

Today, the NFL is divided into two conferences. There is the NFC and the AFC. Each has four divisions of 4 teams. Teams play 16 games during a season.

Each conference has 6 teams that go to the playoffs. These include the 4 division winners and 2 wild card teams. Wild cards go to the teams with the next best records after the division winners.

The wild card games are the first round of the playoffs. The 2 top-ranked teams receive a bye. The bottom 4 teams play. Remaining teams play in the divisional round of the playoffs.

The winners of the divisional round then move on to the conference championship games. These games decide the 2 teams that play in the Super Bowl.

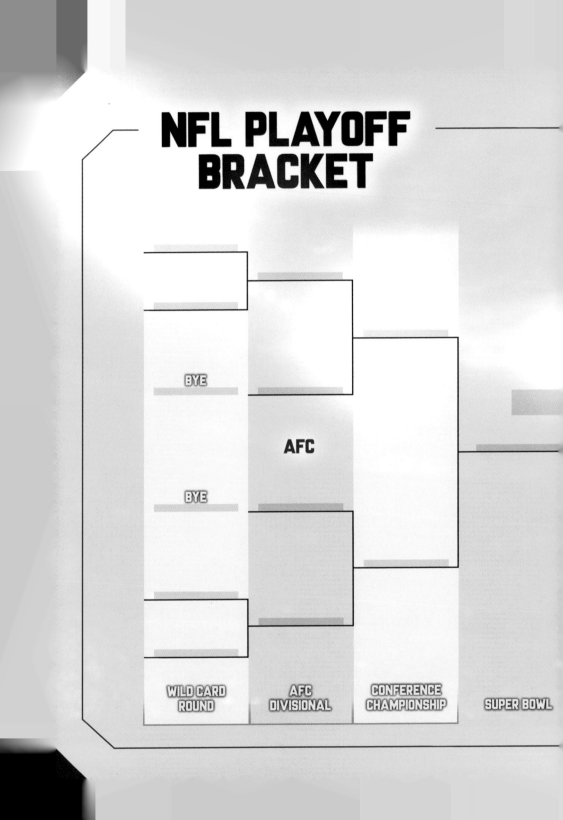

NFL PLAYOFF BRACKET

BYE

BYE

AFC

WILD CARD
ROUND

AFC
DIVISIONAL

CONFERENCE
CHAMPIONSHIP

SUPER BOWL

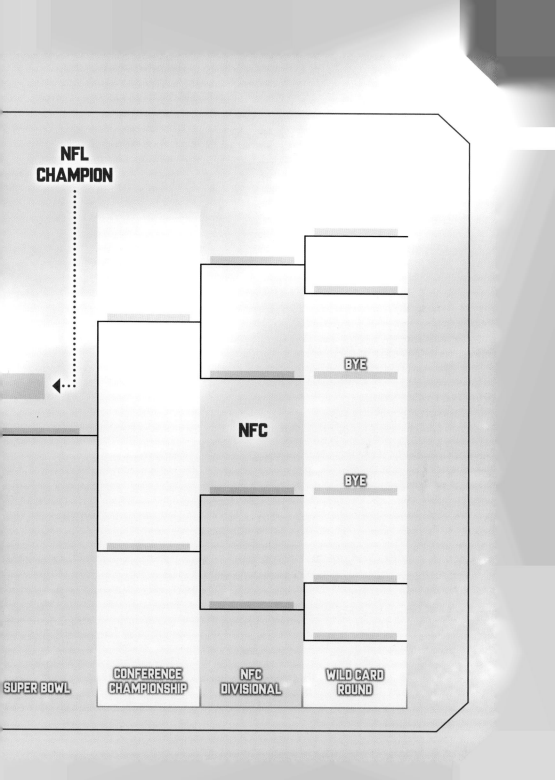

**NFL
CHAMPION**

BYE

BYE

NFC

SUPER BOWL

**CONFERENCE
CHAMPIONSHIP**

**NFC
DIVISIONAL**

**WILD CARD
ROUND**

COMMERCIAL BREAKS

Getting together for the Super Bowl is popular among friends and family. But there is more to watch than just the game. Super Bowl halftime shows feature popular musical performances.

Companies also create their best and funniest ads to air during the big game. Commercials are one of the many reasons fans tune in to watch the Super Bowl!

GLOSSARY

bye—a case in which a team moves to the next round of play without having to play a game

conferences—large groupings of sports teams that often play each other

defensive lineman—a player who tries to stop the offense from moving forward

divisions—small groupings of sports teams; there are usually several divisions of teams in a conference.

fumble—to lose control of the ball while holding it

league—a large group of sports teams that often play each other

playoffs—games played after the regular season is over; playoff games determine which teams play in the Super Bowl.

quarterback—a player on offense whose main job is to throw and hand off the ball

rivals—two or more trying to get what only one can have

stadiums—buildings where sports games are played

wild card—a team selected to fill in the final spots of a playoff tournament

TO LEARN MORE

AT THE LIBRARY

Blaine, Richard. *Cups, Bowls, and Other Football Championships*. New York, N.Y.: Crabtree Publishing Company, 2016.

Doeden, Matt. *The Super Bowl: Chasing Football Immortality*. Minneapolis, Minn.: Millbrook Press, 2018.

Frederick, Shane. *Stars of the Super Bowl*. North Mankato, Minn.: Capstone Press, 2017.

ON THE WEB

Learning more about the Super Bowl is as easy as 1, 2, 3.

1. Go to www.factsurfer.com.

2. Enter "Super Bowl" into the search box.

3. Click the "Surf" button and you will see a list of related web sites.

With factsurfer.com, finding more information is just a click away.

INDEX

The images in this book are reproduced through the courtesy of: Bob Andres/TNS/ Newscom, front cover (athlete); Spencer Allen/Image on Sport/ Newscom, front cover (trophy); John David Mercer/ USA TODAY Sports/ Newscom, pp. 4-5; Elsa/ Getty, pp. 6-7; Perry Knots/ AP Images, p. 8; Focus On Sport/ Getty, pp. 9, 12; James Drake/Sports Illustrated/ Getty, pp. 10-11; Bettmann/ Getty, p. 13; Ric Tapia/ AP Images, pp. 14-15; Kirby Lee/ AP Images, p. 16; Erick W. Rasco/Sports Illustrated/ Getty, p. 17; Abaca Press/Hahn Lionel/Abaca/Sipa USA/ Newscom, p. 20; Chobani/ D5/Splash/ Newscom, p. 21 (television commercial); Monkey Business Images, p. 21 (family).